The Greatest

THE QUOTES OF MUHAMMAD ALI

M. PREFONTAINE

INTRODUCTION

No one has straddled the world of sport, politics and popular culture as Muhammad Ali did.

He was born in Louisville in 1942 in an America where blacks were subjected to a brutal apartheid and were treated as second class citizens. He rose, through his boxing skill and character, to become the most famous person in the world at the time.

He was most famous for styling himself as 'The Greatest'. There is a consensus that he was the greatest of boxers during an era of great boxers. However, he was far more than that. He was a very great man a moral leader, anti-war and fierce opponent of racial prejudice.

A career beyond boxing as a black political leader, fighting for the rights of an oppressed minority, seemed inevitable. Fate had another twist however and Ali suffered from Parkinson's Disease for 30 years, possibly exacerbated by an extended boxing career. This rendered his full potential as an advocate for black rights impossible.

This book tells the story of a much loved and complex man through his own words.

I'll tell you how I would like to be remembered: As a black man who won the heavyweight title - Who was humorous and never looked down on those who looked up to him – A man who stood for freedom, justice and equality – And I wouldn't even mind if folks forgot how pretty I was.

Muhammad Ali

CONTENTS

CHAPTER 1: BOXING

Never put your money against Cassius Clay, for you will never have a lucky day.

~~~

I want 15 referees to be at this fight because there ain't no one man who can keep up with the pace I am gonna set, except me.

~~~

If you sign to fight me, you need speed and endurance but what you need most is to increase your insurance.

~~~

The man who will whip me will be fast, strong and hasn't been born yet.

~~~

I outwit them, and then I outhit them.

~~~

I'm so fast I could hit you before God gets the news.

~~~

When I'm gone, boxing will be nothing again. The fans with the cigars and the hats turned down'll be there, but no more housewives and little men in the street and foreign presidents. It's goin' to be back to the fighter who comes to town, smells a flower, visits a hospital, blows a horn and says he's in shape. Old hat. I was the onliest boxer in history people asked questions like a senator.

~~~

If you even dream of beating me you'd better wake up and apologize.

~~~

I have been so great in boxing they had to create an image like Rocky, a white image on the screen, to counteract my image in the ring. America has to have its white images, no matter where it gets them. Jesus, Wonder Woman, Tarzan and Rocky.

~~~

I figured that if I said it enough, I would convince the world that I really was the greatest.

~~~

Boxing is a lot of white men watching two black men beat each other up.

~~~

My trainer don't tell me nothing between rounds. I don't allow him to. I fight the fight. All I want to know is did I win the round. It's too late for advice.

~~~

People don't realize what they had till it's gone. Like President Kennedy, there was no one like him, the Beatles, and my man Elvis Presley. I was the Elvis of boxing.

~~~

I am the astronaut of boxing. Joe Louis and Dempsey were just jet pilots. I'm in a world of my own.

~~~

They can boo me, yell at me and throw peanuts at me – as long as they pay to get in.

~~~

I never thought of losing, but now that it's happened, the only thing is to do it right. That's my obligation to all the people who believe in me. We all have to take defeats in life.

~~~

No one knows what to say in the loser's locker room.

~~~

I calculate that I took 20,000 punches, but I earned millions and kept a lot of it. I may talk slow, but my mind is OK.

~~~

When I won the Golden Gloves in 1960 that made me realize I had a chance. And when I won at the Olympics that sealed it: I was the champ.

~~~

I always bring out the best in men I fight, but Joe Frazier, I'll tell the world right now, brings out the best in me. I'm gonna tell ya, that's one helluva man, and God bless him.

~~~

I'm so fast that last night I turned off the light switch in my hotel room and was in bed before the room was dark.

It's not bragging if you can back it up.

~~~

It's just a job. Grass grows, birds fly, waves pound the sand. I beat people up.

~~~

I am the greatest, I said that even before I knew I was.

~~~

If you lose a big fight, it will worry you all of your life. It will plague you - until you get your revenge.

~~~

I should be a postage stamp, because that's the only way I'll ever get licked. I'm beautiful. I'm fast. I'm so mean I make medicine sick. I can't possibly be beat.

~~~

I'm not the greatest; I'm the double greatest. Not only do I knock 'em out, I pick the round.

~~~

You can't keep your mind on fighting when you're thinking about a woman. You can't keep your concentration. You feel like sleeping all the time.

~~~

To make America the greatest is my goal, so I beat the Russian and I beat the Pole. And for the U.S.A. won the medal of gold. The Greeks said, 'You're better than the Cassius of old.

~~~

It's hard to be humble, when you're as great as I am.

~~~

Joe Frazier got hit more than me - and he doesn't have Parkinson's.

~~~

Ever since I first came here in 1963 to fight Henry Cooper, I have loved the people of England.

~~~

If I said I would knock out Sonny Liston in 1 minute and 49 seconds of the first round, that would hurt the gate.

~~~

No boxer in the history of boxing has had Parkinson's. There's no injury in my brain that suggests that the illness came from boxing.

~~~

There are no pleasures in a fight but some of my fights have been a pleasure to win.

~~~

I hated every minute of training, but I said, 'Don't quit. Suffer now and live the rest of your life as a champion.

~~~

To be a great champion you must believe you are the best. If you're not, pretend you are.

~~~

Float like a butterfly, sting like a bee. The hands can't hit what the eyes can't see.

~~~

The fight is won or lost far away from the witnesses, behind the lines, in the gym, and out there on the road; long before I dance under those lights.

~~~

I'm the greatest, I'm a bad man, and I'm pretty.

~~~

All through my life, I have been tested. My will has been tested, my courage has been tested, my strength has been tested. Now my patience and endurance are being tested.

~~~

I am the greatest, I'm the greatest that ever lived. I don't have a mark on my face.

~~~

Champions aren't made in the gyms. Champions are made from something they have deep inside them: a desire, a dream, a vision. They have to have last-minute stamina, they have to be a little faster, they have to have the skill and the will. But the will must be stronger than the skill.

~~~

I told you all, all of my critics, that I was the greatest of all time. Never make me the underdog until I'm about 50 years old.

~~~

I'm so fast that last night I turned off the light switch in my hotel room and got into bed before the room was dark.

~~~

When I was 14, and listening to the radio, and I heard the announcer: 'Still champion of the whole world – Rocky Marciano.' I knew I wanted to be champion. He was a big influence.

~~~

I am not the greatest, I'm the double greatest. Not only do I knock 'em out, I pick the round. I'm the boldest, the prettiest, the most superior, most scientific, most skillfullest fighter in the ring today.

~~~

CHAPTER 2: LIFE

I'd like for them to say he took a few cups of love, he took one tablespoon of patience, teaspoon of generosity, one pint of kindness. He took one quart of laughter, one pinch of concern, and then, he mix willingness with happiness, he added lots of faith, and he stirred it up well, then he spreads it over his span of a lifetime, and he served it to each and every deserving person he met.

~~~

What counts in the ring is what you can do after you're exhausted. The same is true of life.

~~~

Friendship... is not something you learn in school. But if you haven't learned the meaning of friendship, you really haven't learned anything.

~~~

He who is not courageous enough to take risks will accomplish nothing in life.

~~~

I know where I'm going and I know the truth, and I don't have to be what you want me to be. I'm free to be what I want.

~~~

I've been everywhere in the world, seen everything, had everything a man can have.

~~~

I shook up the world, I'm the king of the world. You must listen to me. I am the greatest! I can't be beat.

~~~

Silence is golden when you can't think of a good answer.

~~~

We can't be brave without fear.

~~~

I figure I'll be champ for about ten years and then I'll let my brother take over - like the Kennedys down in Washington.

~~~

Only a man who knows what it is like to be defeated can reach down to the bottom of his soul and come up with the extra ounce of power it takes to win when the match is even.

~~~

The fact is, I was never too bright in school. I ain't ashamed of it, though. I mean, how much do school principals make a month?

~~~

The man who views the world at 50 the same as he did at 20 has wasted 30 years of his life.

~~~

To be able to give away riches is mandatory if you wish to possess them. This is the only way that you will be truly rich.

~~~

What keeps me going is goals.

~~~

I said I was 'The Greatest,' I never said I was the smartest.

~~~

Old age is just a record of one's whole life.

~~~

It's the repetition of affirmations that leads to belief. And once that belief becomes a deep conviction, things begin to happen.

~~~

If they can make penicillin out of moldy bread, they can sure make something out of you.

~~~

Wars of nations are fought to change maps. But wars of poverty are fought to map change.

~~~

My only fault is that I don't realize how great I really am.

~~~

At home I am a nice guy: but I don't want the world to know. Humble people, I've found, don't get very far.

~~~

Anywhere I go, there is always an incredible crowd that follows me. In Rome, as I land at the airport, even the men kiss me. I love Rome.

~~~

I'm the most recognized and loved man that ever lived cuz there weren't no satellites when Jesus and Moses were around, so people far away in the villages didn't know about them.

~~~

I've made my share of mistakes along the way, but if I have changed even one life for the better, I haven't lived in vain.

~~~

I'm the greatest thing that ever lived! I'm the king of the world! I'm a bad man. I'm the prettiest thing that ever lived.

~~~

My way of joking is to tell the truth. That's the funniest joke in the world.

~~~

It isn't the mountains ahead to climb that wear you out; it's the pebble in your shoe.

~~~

It's lack of faith that makes people afraid of meeting challenges, and I believed in myself.

~~~

I'm a poet, I'm a prophet, I'm the resurrector, I'm the savior of the boxing world. If it wasn't for me, the game would be dead.

~~~

Impossible is just a big word thrown around by small men who find it easier to live in the world they've been given than to explore the power they have to change it. Impossible is not a fact. It's an opinion. Impossible is not a declaration. It's a dare. Impossible is potential. Impossible is temporary. Impossible is nothing.

~~~

I wish people would love everybody else the way they love me. It would be a better world.

~~~

My principles are more important than the
money or my title.

~~~

Service to others is the rent you pay for your
room here on earth.

~~~

Don't count the days, make the days count.

~~~

I am an ordinary man who worked hard to
develop the talent I was given. I believed in
myself, and I believe in the goodness of others.

~~~

A man who views the world the same at fifty as he
did at twenty has wasted thirty years of his life.

~~~

I wanted to use my fame and this face that
everyone knows so well to help uplift and inspire
people around the world.

~~~

There are more pleasant things to do than beat up people.

~~~

If my mind can conceive it, and my heart can believe it - then I can achieve it.

~~~

I'm a fighter. I believe in the eye-for-an-eye business. I'm no cheek turner. I got no respect for a man who won't hit back. You kill my dog, you better hide your cat.

~~~

Live everyday as if it were your last because someday you're going to be right.

~~~

The best way to make your dreams come true is to wake up.

~~~

What you're thinking is what you're becoming.

~~~

The man with no imagination has no wings.

~~~

Inside of a ring or out, ain't nothing wrong with going down. It's staying down that's wrong.

~~~

Life is a gamble. You can get hurt, but people die in plane crashes, lose their arms and legs in car accidents; people die every day. Same with fighters: some die, some get hurt, some go on. You just don't let yourself believe it will happen to you.

~~~

I am America. I am the part you won't recognize. But get used to me. Black, confident, cocky; my name, not yours; my religion, not yours; my goals, my own; get used to me.

~~~

You lose nothing when fighting for a cause ... In my mind the losers are those who don't have a cause they care about.

~~~

Age is whatever you think it is. You are as old as you think you are

~~~

Others may know pleasure, but pleasure is not happiness. It has no more importance than a shadow following a man.

~~~

I try not to speak about all the charities and people I help, because I believe we can only be truly generous when we expect nothing in return.

~~~

I want to get out with my greatness intact.

~~~

Wisdom is knowing when you can't be wise.

~~~

You know I hate fighting. If I knew how to make a living some other way, I would.

~~~

The greatest victory in life is to rise above the material things that we once valued most.

~~~

Life is short; we get old so fast. It doesn't make sense to waste time on hating.

~~~

I may not talk perfect white talk-type English, but I give you wisdom.

~~~

Braggin' is when a person says something and can't do it. I do what I say.

~~~

I'm so mean, I make medicine sick.

~~~

If there is no enemy within, the enemy outside can do you no harm.

~~~

Life is like a boxing match defeat is not declared when you fall, but when you refuse to stand back up.

~~~

My toughest fight was with my first wife.

~~~

Love is a net that catches hearts like a fish.

~~~

Give up what appears to be doubtful for what is certain. Truth brings peace of mind, and deception doubt.

~~~

When a chivalrous man makes an oath, he is faithful to it, and when he attains power, he spares his enemy.

~~~

You don't want no pie in the sky when you die, you want something here on the ground while you're still around.

~~~

Life is like a boxing match defeat is not declared when you fall, but when you refuse to stand back up.

~~~

If your dreams don't scare you, then they are not big enough.

~~~

I don't count my sit ups. I only start counting when it starts hurting. That is when I start counting, because then it really counts. That's what makes you a champion.

~~~

Fighting by itself doesn't interest me anymore. I want to help people, the black people and I need any kind of media to spread my thought: God, charity, peace.

~~~

I don't know how many millions I'll make, so I have to give some back to charity. God blesses me with the money, but only if I give some away.

~~~

Success is not achieved by winning all the time. Real success comes when we rise after we fall. Some mountains are higher than others. Some roads steeper than the next. There are hardships and setbacks but you cannot let them stop you. Even on the steepest road you must not turn back.

~~~

This life is not real. I conquered the world and it did not bring me satisfaction.

~~~

Whatever the challenge was, however unattainable the goal may have seemed, I never let anyone talk me out of believing in myself.

~~~

Every day is different, and some days are better than others, but no matter how challenging the day, I get up and live it.

~~~

My soul has grown over the years, and some of my views have changed. As long as I am alive, I will continue to try to understand more because the work of the heart is never done.

~~~

I'll tell you how I would like to be remembered:
As a black man who won the heavyweight title -
Who was humorous and never looked down on
those who looked up to him – A man who stood
for freedom, justice and equality – And I wouldn't
even mind if folks forgot how pretty I was.

~~~

CHAPTER 3: RELIGION

The word 'Islam' means 'peace.' The word 'Muslim' means 'one who surrenders to God.' But the press makes us seem like haters.

~~~

Allah's the Arabic term for God. Stand up for God, fight for God, work for God and do the right thing, and go the right way, things will end up in your corner.

~~~

I'm no leader; I'm a little humble follower.

~~~

Terrorists are not following Islam. Killing people and blowing up people and dropping bombs in places and all this is not the way to spread the word of Islam. So people realize now that all Muslims are not terrorists.

~~~

Rivers, ponds, lakes and streams - they all have different names, but they all contain water. Just as religions do - they all contain truths.

~~~

It's a lack of faith that makes people afraid of meeting challenges, and I believed in myself.

~~~

A rooster crows only when it sees the light. Put him in the dark and he'll never crow. I have seen the light and I'm crowing.

~~~

God's got me here for something. I can feel it. I was born for everything that I'm doing now.

~~~

I'm just hoping that people understand that Islam is peace and not violence.

~~~

I believe in the religion of Islam. I believe in Allah and peace.

~~~

Allah is the Greatest. I'm just the greatest boxer

~~~

Truly great people in history never wanted to be great for themselves. All they wanted was the chance to do good for others and be close to God.

~~~

I'd rather be punished here in this life than the hereafter.

~~~

I am a Muslim and there is nothing Islamic about killing innocent people in Paris, San Bernardino, or anywhere else in the world. True Muslims know that the ruthless violence of so called Islamic Jihadists goes against the very tenets of our religion.

~~~

The Nation Of Islam taught that white people are devils. I don't believe that now; in fact, I never really believed that.

~~~

Our political leaders should use their position to bring understanding about the religion of Islam and clarify that these misguided murderers have perverted people's views on what Islam really is.

~~~

And if God ever calls me to a holy war, I want Joe (Frazier) fighting beside me.

~~~

I have not lost [Allah's] hope in us to show compassion where none exists and to extend mercy in the most difficult of circumstances. We as Muslims must lead by example.

~~~

I'm not afraid of dying. I have faith; I do everything I can to live my life right; and I believe that dying will bring me closer to God.

~~~

Parkinson's is my toughest fight. No, it doesn't hurt. It's hard to explain. I'm being tested to see if I will keep praying, to see if I will keep my faith. All great people are tested by God.

~~~

Maybe Parkinson's is God's way of reminding me what is important. It slowed me down and caused me to listen rather than talk. People pay more attention to me now because I don't talk so much.

~~~

Most people don't pray until they're in trouble. When people need help they pray a lot. But after they get what they want, they slow down. If a man takes five showers a day, his body will be clean. Praying five times a day helps me clean my mind.

~~~

I don't smoke but I keep a match box in my pocket, when my heart slips towards sin, I burn the matchstick and heat my palm with it, then say to myself, "Ali you can't even bear this heat, how would you bear the unbearable heat of hellfire"?

~~~

I'm a Muslim. I've been a Muslim for 20 years. . .. You know me. I'm a boxer. I've been called the greatest. People recognize me for being a boxer and a man of truth. I wouldn't be here representing Islam if it were terrorist. . .. I think all people should know the truth, come to recognize the truth. Islam is peace.

~~~

Chapter 4: Racism

Cassius Clay is a name that white people gave to my slave master. Now that I am free, that I don't belong anymore to anyone, that I'm not a slave anymore, I gave back their white name, and I chose a beautiful African one.

~~~

When you can whip any man in the world, you never know peace.

~~~

Hating people because of their color is wrong. And it doesn't matter which color does the hating. It's just plain wrong.

~~~

White people just don't want their slaves to be free. That's the whole thing.

~~~

I know I got it made while the masses of black people are catchin' hell, but as long as they ain't free, I ain't free.

~~~

I had to prove you could be a new kind of black man. I had to show the world.

~~~

Prejudice comes from being in the dark; sunlight disinfects it.

~~~

It don't seem possible, but 28 million people run this country and not one white man is involved. I used to think that Africans were savages. But now I am here I have learnt that many Africans are wiser than we are.
On arrival in Zaire for 'The Rumble in the Jungle'.

~~~

My gloves are going to jail. They ain't done nothin' — yet.

~~~

You lose nothing when fighting for a cause ... In my mind the losers are those who don't have a cause they care about.

~~~

When I meet a new person, I don't see race or religion. I look deeper. We must learn to satisfy our conflicts peacefully and to respect one another.

~~~

CHAPTER 5: VIETNAM WAR

I didn't want to submit to the army and then, on the day of judgment, have God say to me, 'Why did you do that?' This life is a trial, and you realize that what you do is going to be written down for Judgment Day.

~~~

Why should they ask me to put on a uniform and go 10,000 miles from home and drop bombs and bullets on Brown people in Vietnam while so-called Negro people in Louisville are treated like dogs and denied simple human rights? No I'm not going 10,000 miles from home to help murder and burn another poor nation simply to continue the domination of white slave masters of the darker people the world over. This is the day when such evils must come to an end. I have been warned that to take such a stand would cost me millions of dollars. But I have said it once and I will say it again. The real enemy of my people is here. I will not disgrace my religion, my people or myself by becoming a tool to enslave those who are fighting for their own justice, freedom and equality. If I thought the war was going to bring freedom and equality to 22 million of my people they wouldn't have to draft me, I'd join tomorrow. I have nothing to lose by standing up for my beliefs. So I'll go to jail, so what? We've been in jail for 400 years.

~~~

I ain't got no quarrel with The Vietcong...no Vietcong ever called me Nigger.

~~~

People say I talk so slow today. That's no surprise. I calculated I've taken 29,000 punches. But I earned $57m and I saved half of it. So I took a few hard knocks. Do you know how many black men are killed every year by guns and knives without a penny to their names? I may talk slow, but my mind is OK.

~~~

It's like a man been in chains all his life and suddenly the chains are taken off. He's doesn't realise he is free until he gets all the circulation back in his legs and starts to feel his fingers.
After the Supreme Court quashed his conviction for draft evasion.

~~~

I strongly object to the fact that so many newspapers have given the American public and the world the impression that I have only two alternatives in taking this stand: either I go to jail or go to the Army. There is another alternative and that alternative is justice. If justice prevails, if my Constitutional rights are upheld, I will be forced to go neither to the Army nor jail. In the end I am confident that justice will come my way for the truth must eventually prevail.

~~~

There is one hell of a difference between fighting in the ring and going to war in Vietnam.

~~~

Chapter 6: Opponents

You've got to give him credit – he put up a good fight for one and a half rounds.

~~~

I done wrestled with an alligator, I done tussled with a whale; handcuffed lightning, thrown thunder in jail; only last week, I murdered a rock, injured a stone, hospitalized a brick; I'm so mean I make medicine sick.

~~~

Why, chump, I bet you scare yourself to death just starin' in the mirror. You ugly bear. You never fought nobody but tramps and has-beens. You call yourself a world champion? You're too old and slow to be a champion.
Before fighting Sonny Liston

~~~

He was supposed to kill me. Well I am still alive.
On beating Sonny Liston

~~~

Joe Frazier is so ugly that when he cries, the tears turn around and go down the back of his head.

~~~

Frazier is so ugly that he should donate his face to the U.S. Bureau of Wild Life.

~~~

Joe Frazier is the greatest of all time, next to me.

~~~

Sonny Liston is nothing. The man can't talk. The man can't fight. The man needs talking lessons. The man needs boxing lessons. And since he's gonna fight me, he needs falling lessons.

~~~

It will be a killer, and a chiller, and a thriller, when I get the gorilla in Manila.

~~~

I've seen George Foreman shadow boxing, and the shadow won.

~~~

Ali's got a left, Ali's got a right - when he knocks you down, you'll sleep for the night; and when you lie on the floor and the ref counts to ten, hope and pray that you never meet me again.

~~~

You think the world was shocked when Nixon resigned? Wait till I whup George Foreman's behind.

~~~

I'll beat him so bad he'll need a shoehorn to put his hat on.

~~~

That all you got, George?
Ali taunts George Foreman, in the rope-a-dope fight in Zaire in 1974.

~~~

..now Clay swings with a right, what a beautiful swing And raises the bear straight out of the ring; Liston is rising and the ref wears a frown For he can't start counting 'til Liston comes down; Now Liston disappears from view, the crowd is getting frantic But our radar stations have picked him up somewhere over the Atlantic; Who would have thought when they came to the fight That they'd witness the launching of a human satellite? Yes the crowd did not dream when they laid down

their money That they would see a total eclipse of the Sonny.

~~~

He's (Sonny Liston) too ugly to be the world champ. The world champ should be pretty like me.

~~~

Get up sucker and fight. Get up and fight.
Ali taunts Liston during their second fight in 1965

~~~

What's my name, fool? What's my name?
Ali taunts Ernie Terrell, who had refused to acknowledge Ali's change of name before their bout in 1967

~~~

I saw your wife. You're not as dumb as you look.
To Joe Frazier

~~~

CHAPTER 7: QUOTES ABOUT ALI.

The world's greatest athlete is in danger of being our most beautiful man. Women draw an audible breath. Men look down...for he is the Prince of Heaven.
Norman Mailer

~~~

In boxing, I had a lot of fear. Fear was good. But, for the first time, in the bout with Muhammad Ali, I didn't have any fear. I thought, 'This is easy. This is what I've been waiting for'. No fear at all. No nervousness. And I lost.
George Foreman

~~~

That was always the difference between Muhammad Ali and the rest of us. He came, he saw, and if he didn't entirely conquer - he came as close as anybody we are likely to see in the lifetime of this doomed generation.
Hunter S. Thompson

~~~

Muhammad Ali was the kind of guy you either loved or hated, but you wanted to see him. I

happen to really love him. He brought boxing to another level and always made you laugh.
Gerry Cooney

~~~

If you're a person struggling to eat and stay healthy, you might have heard about Michael Jordan or Muhammad Ali, but you'll never have heard of Bill Gates.
Bill Gates

~~~

You get these moments in the ring that live forever. That's what Muhammad Ali accomplished, and I hope that I have, too.
Sugar Ray Leonard

~~~

Muhammad Ali was a god, an idol and an icon. He was boxing. Any kid that had the opportunity to talk to Ali, to get advice from Muhammad Ali, was privileged. He's always given me time to ask questions, although I was so in awe that I didn't ask questions.
Sugar Ray Leonard

~~~

Muhammad Ali - he was a magnificent fighter and he was an icon... Every head must bow, every knee must bend, every tongue must confess, thou art the greatest, the greatest of all time, Muhammad, Muhammad Ali.
Don King

~~~

Muhammad Ali is a true hero, and the fact there's something wrong with him is his badge of valour. He's a great man.
George Foreman

~~~

In fifty years of covering the sport, of course Muhammad Ali is by far the dominant figure.
Dick Schaap

~~~

I'd see people being really successful, whether it was my teammates or big-name fighters like Muhammad Ali and Mike Tyson, and I'd think, 'I want to be a legend like that'.
Holly Holm

~~~

Muhammad Ali shook up the world. And the world is better for it
Barack Obama.

~~~

To put him as a boxer is an injustice.
George Foreman.

~~~

Muhammad Ali was not just a champion in the ring - he was a champion of civil rights, and a role model for so many people.
David Cameron

~~~

Muhammad Ali was one of the greatest human beings I have ever met. No doubt he was one of the best people to have lived in this day and age.
George Foreman

~~~

His fight outside the ring would cost him his title and his public standing. It would earn him enemies on the left and the right, make him reviled, and nearly send him to jail. But Ali stood his ground. And his victory helped us get used to the America we recognize today.
Barack Obama

~~~

At a time when blacks who spoke up about injustice were labelled uppity and often arrested under one pretext or another, Muhammad willingly sacrificed the best years of his career to stand tall and fight for what he believed was right. In doing so, he made all Americans, black and white, stand taller. I may be 7ft 2in but I never felt taller than when standing in his shadow.
Kareem Abdul-Jabbar

~~~

There will never be another Muhammad Ali. The black community all around the world, black people all around the world, needed him. He was the voice for us. He's the voice for me to be where I'm at today.
Floyd Mayweather

~~~

We lost a giant today. Boxing benefitted from Muhammad Ali's talents but not as much as mankind benefitted from his humanity.
Manny Pacquiao

~~~

He was the greatest fighter of all time but his boxing career is secondary to his contribution to

the world. He's the most transforming figure of my time certainly. He did more to change race relations and the views of people than even Martin Luther King.
Bob Arum

~~~

Ali, the G-O-A-T [Greatest Of All Time]. A giant, an inspiration, a man of peace, a warrior for the cure. Thank you.
Michael J Fox

~~~

Muhammad Ali was the greatest, not only an extraordinary athlete but a man of great courage and humanity.
Bernie Sanders

~~~

God came for his champion. So long great one. Muhammad Ali, The Greatest. RIP.
Mike Tyson

~~~

Not only a very sad loss for boxing, but for the whole of sport as he was quite simply the greatest and most iconic athlete the world has ever known.
Ricky Hatton

~~~

Printed in Germany
by Amazon Distribution
GmbH, Leipzig